A BLUE BANNER
BIOGRAPHY

Miguel Tejada

Joanne Mattern

Mitchell Lane
PUBLISHERS

P.O. Box 196
Hockessin, Delaware 19707
Visit us on the web: www.mitchelllane.com
Comments? email us: mitchelllane@mitchelllane.com

SEAFORD, NEW YORK 11783

Printing   1   2   3   4   5   6   7   8   9

Blue Banner Biographies

Alicia Keys	Allen Iverson	Alan Jackson
Ashanti	Ashlee Simpson	Ashton Kutcher
Avril Lavigne	Beyoncé	Bow Wow
Britney Spears	Christina Aguilera	Christopher Paul Curtis
Clay Aiken	Condoleezza Rice	Daniel Radcliffe
Derek Jeter	Eminem	Eve
50-Cent	Gwen Stefani	Ice Cube
Jamie Foxx	Ja Rule	Jay-Z
Jennifer Lopez	J. K. Rowling	Jodie Foster
Justin Berfield	Kate Hudson	Kelly Clarkson
Kenny Chesney	Lance Armstrong	Lindsay Lohan
Mariah Carey	Mario	Mary-Kate and Ashley Olsen
Melissa Gilbert	Michael Jackson	**Miguel Tejada**
Missy Elliott	Nelly	Orlando Bloom
Paris Hilton	P. Diddy	Peyton Manning
Queen Latifah	Rita Williams-Garcia	Ritchie Valens
Ron Howard	Rudy Giuliani	Sally Field
Selena	Shirley Temple	Tim McGraw
Usher		

Library of Congress Cataloging-in-Publication Data
Mattern, Joanne, 1963–
    Miguel Tejada / by Joanne Mattern
        p. cm. — (Blue banner biographies)
    Includes bibliographical references and index.
    ISBN 1-58415-505-1 (lib. bdg. : alk. paper)
    1. Tejada, Miguel, 1976– Juvenile literature. 2. Baseball players— Dominican Republic —
Biography — Juvenile literature. I. Title. II. Blue banner biography.
GV865.T45M38 2006
796.357092 — dc22   2005036691

ISBN-10: 1-58415-505-1   ISBN-13: 978-1-58415-505-8

ABOUT THE AUTHOR: Joanne Mattern is the author of more than 100 nonfiction books for children. Along with biographies, she has written extensively about animals, nature, history, sports, and foreign cultures. She wrote *Brian McBride* and *Peyton Manning* for Mitchell Lane Publishers. She lives near New York City with her husband and three young daughters.

PHOTO CREDITS: Cover—Jamie Squire/Getty Images; p. 4—John G. Mabanglo/AFP/Getty Images; pp. 6, 9—Sharon Beck; p. 7—Paul Buck/AFP/Getty Images; p. 11—Ezra Shaw/Getty Images; p. 14—Jeff Carlick/Getty Images; p. 17—Mike Fiala/AFP/Getty Images; p. 18—Otto Gruele Jr./Getty Images; p. 21—Tom Hauck/Allsport/Getty Images; p. 22—Brian Bahr/Getty Images; p. 25—Win McNamee/Getty Images; p. 27—Elsa/Getty Images; p. 28—Elise Amendola/AP Photo.

PLB

CONTENTS

While he was shortstop for the Oakland A's, Miguel Tejada showed his grace and power as he jumped over Ed Sprague of the Boston Red Sox to complete a double play. The A's went on to win this July 2000 game, 5-2.

Most Valuable Player

*I*t was November 2002. Miguel Tejada had just finished a thrilling baseball season. His team, the Oakland Athletics, had won 103 games. They had won 20 games in a row. That was a new record for an American League team. Tejada played shortstop for the Athletics, who were also called the A's. He was one of the most exciting players on the team. Tejada hit lots of home runs. He drove in many runs for his team. He made stunning defensive plays in the field, too.

Every year, Major League Baseball picks two Most Valuable Players, or MVPs. One player is from the National League. The other player is from the American League. Many people thought Tejada might be the American League MVP. Many others felt another shortstop, Alex Rodriguez, would win.

Miguel Tejada was home in Baní, a town in the Dominican Republic. One night he was playing dominoes with his friends. The phone rang. Tejada's agent Diego Benz

A map of the Dominican Republic. Tejada was born in Baní, in the southern part of the country.

was calling. He had great news. Tejada had been picked as the American League MVP!

Tejada's friends and family cheered and yelled. Tejada was surprised. "Are you sure?" he asked Diego. "I can't believe it!"

Everyone in the Dominican Republic was happy that Tejada had won. The president of the Dominican Republic invited him to a special party. Miguel brought two busloads of his family and friends to meet the president. He was very excited. "This is the first time I have been to the presidential palace," he said. "This is a happy time for me. All people from my country deserve this."

The Dominican Republic is very proud of Miguel Tejada. Tejada is very proud of his country. Even though he is a rich and famous baseball star, he has never forgotten where he came from. Miguel Tejada's story is an amazing journey.

After Tejada forces out Texas Ranger Frank Catalanotto at second base, he throws the bull to first to make a double play.

A Difficult Childhood

Miguel Odalis Tejada was born on May 25, 1976, in Baní, the Dominican Republic. About 100,000 people live in Baní. The town is about 40 miles from Santo Domingo, the capital of the Dominican Republic.

Miguel's mother was Mora. His father is Daniel. Mora and Daniel already had seven children by the time Miguel was born.

Miguel was a skinny, sickly baby. "When I was born I was ugly, ugly, ugly," he later said. "My father said they thought I was going to die, that I looked like I was sick."

The Tejadas were very poor. Mora Tejada cleaned houses. She worked as a cook too. Daniel Tejada worked in construction. The older children also worked. Miguel's sisters cleaned and cooked like their mother. His brothers shined shoes or worked with their father.

When Miguel was three years old, disaster struck the Dominican Republic. A big storm, Hurricane David, hit the island on August 31, 1979. The storm killed hundreds of

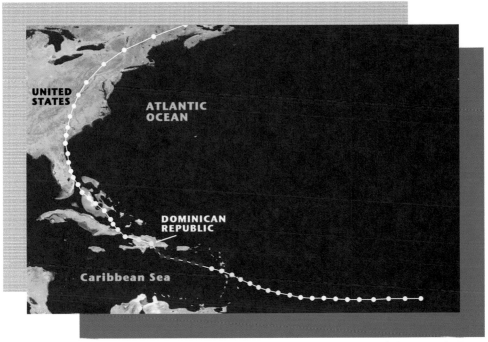

The path of Hurricane David. In 1979, this storm devastated the Dominican Republic, killing hundreds and leaving thousands of people homeless.

people there. It destroyed thousands of houses. The Tejadas survived, but their house was one of those demolished by the storm. The family lost everything they had. They had no clothes, no food, and no place to live.

Miguel and his family were homeless for about two weeks. Then they lived in a refugee camp. Finally, the Tejadas found a place to live in Baní. Their new home was in a slum called Los Barrancones. The home was a tiny shack. It had no running water. It had no lights or electricity.

Miguel started school when he was five years old. However, he did not go to school every day. Like most children in Baní, he had to work. Miguel set up a shoeshine stand in the streets of Baní. He gave whatever money he made to his older brothers. They used the money to buy food for the family.

The people in Los Barrancones had a hard life. However, there were good things about living there. Everyone knew and helped one another. People often sat outside their homes and talked. They played music. They shared food and laughter. Most of all, they played baseball.

Baseball was the most popular sport in the Dominican Republic. Children in every town played in the streets and fields. Their balls were made of rolled-up rags. Their bats were tree branches. Gloves were made out of old milk cartons. Miguel never held a real baseball until he was twelve years old. Still, he and his friends played as much as they could.

Miguel learned to play baseball from his older brother, Juansito. When he was a little boy, Juansito had been a fantastic baseball player. Many people thought he would play in the major leagues someday. Then he broke his leg. The family could not afford to send for a doctor. Juansito's leg did not heal straight, and he walked with a limp. His dreams of a baseball career were over.

Miguel spent every spare minute he had playing baseball. He even skipped school to play. By the time he was eleven years old, he was finished with school anyway. His family needed him to work. Miguel worked at a clothing factory. Even after long hours at work, he was ready to play baseball.

Many major-league baseball teams sent scouts to the Dominican Republic. Their job was to find boys who had talent and teach them how to play better baseball. When the boys were seventeen years old, a lucky few might be offered a contract to play baseball in the United States. Miguel dreamed of being one of those boys.

A boy plays baseball in the Dominican Republic. Many Dominican children play baseball and dream of a career in the major leagues.

Then Miguel suffered another tragedy. When he was thirteen years old, his mother became very sick. On December 21, 1989, she died. Miguel was heartbroken. For a while, he did not want to play baseball. He did not want to do anything.

Then things got worse. Miguel's father had to move to another town to find work. Juansito moved away too. Miguel and his sixteen-year-old brother, Denio, were all alone. Sometimes they did not have enough to eat. Miguel felt lonelier than he ever had before.

Slowly, Miguel thought about baseball again. He started to play. He found he still enjoyed the game. Once again, Miguel dreamed of a major-league career.

Someone to Count On

*I*n 1990, Miguel met Enrique Soto. Soto was a scout for the Oakland Athletics. He ran a baseball camp in Baní. He looked for boys who had talent and the will to succeed. One of those boys was Miguel.

It didn't take long for Soto to ask Miguel to train with him. Soto said, "I never had any doubts about his baseball talent. But I did have doubts about him."

Soto was right to worry. Miguel was not used to following rules. He did not like Soto telling him what to do. Miguel started to show up late to practice. He argued with Soto. He spent more time fooling around than he did learning baseball skills.

Finally, Soto had enough. He told Miguel to leave the camp. Miguel went home crying. The next day he came back to camp. He begged Soto to give him another chance. Soto agreed. However, Miguel still had a lot to learn.

Soto was very tough on Miguel. "I think anyone from the outside would have thought I didn't like him or was cruel to him," Soto later said. "But I behaved that way because that's what Miguel needed. He needed me to be hard, so I was hard."

Soto gave Miguel the guidance he did not have at home. The teenager knew that he had to follow Soto's rules. If he did, Miguel knew he would have a chance to join the big leagues. So Miguel worked hard to be a good baseball player.

He could hardly wait until he turned seventeen years old. Seventeen was the age when Dominican players could sign a contract with an American team.

Finally, the big day arrived. The Oakland A's had sent Juan Marichal, a Hall of Fame pitcher, to the Dominican Republic as a scout. Soto had told Marichal's assistants that the A's should sign Miguel. However, the A's were not so sure. Finally, a few weeks after Miguel's seventeenth birthday, the team took a chance. They offered Miguel a contract to play in the United States. Miguel would play in the minor leagues. The team paid him $2,000 to sign with them. That was more money than Miguel had ever seen in his life. He quickly said yes. Then he used the money to buy new clothes and furniture for his family.

In the summer of 1993, Miguel got on a plane to the United States. He was about to start a new life with the Oakland A's. Miguel was ready to make his dreams come true.

Tejada played for the Oakland Athletics' major-league team from 1997 to 2003.

A Star on the Rise

*T*he A's sent Tejada to Medford, Oregon. Medford was the home of the Athletics' minor-league team. This team was the first step for players who hoped to be in the major leagues.

Tejada knew that life in the United States would be hard. He spoke little English. His culture was also very different from that of players who had grown up in the United States. Tejada knew that some Americans would think he was not smart because he could not speak English. He decided he had to be tough. "When I went to Medford I decided I wasn't going to be the kind of person who was always asking for help," he said. "When you do, the Americans speak badly of you." He also decided he would be cheerful and make the most of this wonderful opportunity. He tried not to show that he was really homesick and scared.

Tejada traveled all over the northwestern part of the United States that summer. He played baseball almost every day. His body grew stronger, and he learned many important skills.

Along with baseball skills, Tejada was learning about life. Enrique Soto had told him that a lot of players from the Dominican Republic and other Latin American countries get into trouble when they move to America. The young men are overwhelmed by the money and fun times they can have in the United States. They lose their focus on playing good baseball. Tejada did not want this to happen to him. Everyone soon saw that he always behaved well. He was respectful, and he worked hard.

Tejada played on minor-league teams for the Oakland A's for four years. He spent his summers in the United States. When the baseball season ended, he went home to the Dominican Republic. There, he trained with Enrique Soto and other baseball players. He also played for a team called the Aguilas (AH-gee-lahs). The Aguilas play in a league with other teams from the Dominican Republic. Tejada also played in the Caribbean World Series against teams from several other countries. He liked playing winter ball. He knew playing all year was good for his game. "Playing winter ball every year is why I'm becoming a good player," he once said. "Anything I'm doing wrong in the season, I go back to the Dominican and fix it."

In 1997, Tejada was playing for Oakland's minor-league team in Huntsville, Alabama. No one expected him to reach the major leagues for another year or so. However, Tejada had other ideas. That summer, he hit 22 home runs. He drove in 97 runs. He played so well that the Oakland A's decided Tejada was ready.

In August, Tejada got the call he'd been waiting for. He was on his way to Oakland. He was on his way to the big leagues!

Ruben Rivera of the San Diego Padres slides into second base as Tejada leaps over his head.

Tejada is strong offensively as well as defensively. In 2004 his batting average reached a career high of .311.

Oakland Superstar

*T*ejada played 26 games for the Oakland A's in 1997. Sometimes, it looked like he still had a lot to learn. He had trouble hitting major-league pitches. He made mistakes in the field too. At the end of September, his batting average was just .202. Still, he was a popular player. He was not afraid to go after balls on the field. Oakland decided Tejada would be their starting shortstop in 1998.

In February 1998, Tejada went to Arizona. He practiced at the Oakland A's training camp. He could hardly wait for the season to start.

Then, on March 21, an accident happened. Tejada broke his hand when he caught a ground ball. He could not play for many weeks. He would miss the beginning of the season.

Tejada was sad. However, he worked hard to get his hand back in shape. By the end of May, his hand was healed. In his first few games with the A's, he hit two doubles. He batted in three runs. It was clear that Miguel Tejada was there to stay.

Tejada had great seasons with the A's in 1998 and 1999. In 1999, the team came within three wins of the playoffs. In 2000, another great year, the A's averaged five runs per game. Tejada was batting .275. The A's signed him to a new contract. Over the next four years, he would earn more than $11 million. The team manager, Art Howe, said that Tejada was "one of the main ingredients in our lineup. He's not afraid to be up there with the game on the line. He likes to be in that situation."

The other Oakland players liked having Tejada around. He wasn't just a good player. He was a lot of fun! "He's fun because he gets so excited," said his teammate Mark Ellis.

Tejada and his teammates worked hard. The Oakland A's became a very good team. In 2000, they made it to the division playoffs, and in 2001 they took the wild card spot. However, the New York Yankees beat the team both years to go on to play for the league championships.

Tejada wanted his team to do better in 2002. He knew he would have to do better too. During the winter, he practiced hard. He watched hours of videos of himself playing ball. He worked on ways to hit and field better. When spring training came in 2002, Tejada was ready.

That year, Tejada was a team leader. His batting average was over .300 during the first few months of the season. He made the All-Star team in July. He told a reporter, "Making the All-Star team makes me want to be a better player."

After the All-Star break, Tejada had a 24-game hitting streak. By September he was one of the league's leaders in batting and RBIs. He finished the season with a .308 batting average. He hit 34 home runs and had 131 RBIs. Tejada was great in the field too. One night a scout from another team watched Tejada turn a double play. The scout said, "It's one of his 'Did-you-see-THAT?' plays."

Tejada dives for a ball in an April 2001 game against the Texas Rangers.

Once again, the A's made it to the division playoffs. They played the Minnesota Twins. Everyone thought the A's would win the series. However, the Twins beat them, 5 games to 4.

Tejada went home to the Dominican Republic. He was disappointed that the A's had not made it to the World Series. However, just a few weeks later, he received fantastic news. He had been named the Most Valuable Player in the American League! Tejada was shocked. He had expected Alex Rodriguez to win. Rodriguez was the shortstop for the Texas Rangers.

By the end of 2002, Tejada had achieved many of his goals. He told a magazine reporter, "I've been working all my life for this. I didn't work just to be in the majors. I want to be somebody."

Winning the Home Run Derby in 2004 is one of the many highlights in Tejada's career.

Flying High

*I*n 2003, Tejada had another good year with the
Oakland A's. He was thrilled when the A's won the
division title. However, the team lost the American League
championship to the Boston Red Sox. Once again, Tejada
would not be going to the World Series.

Tejada's contract with the A's ended that year. On
December 14, 2003, he signed a six-year contract with the
Baltimore Orioles. He would be paid $72 million. The
Orioles were not a strong team. They hoped that by adding
good players like Tejada, the team would get better. Tejada
was determined to help the team do well.

Although Baltimore did not make it to the playoffs in
2004, Tejada had a fantastic year. During the first half of the
season, he batted over .300. Then it was time for the All-Star
Game. One of the most exciting parts of the All-Star break is
the Home Run Derby. Tejada had a lot of fun in that
contest! There were many powerful hitters in the derby,
including the legendary Barry Bonds. Tejada outshone them

all. He won the contest with 27 homers. That was a new record!

Tejada continued to shine. At the end of the season, he led the major leagues with 150 RBIs. That and his batting average of .311 and 34 home runs earned him a Silver Slugger Award for shortstop.

Tejada's great baseball was not his only contribution to the Orioles. He also gave the team energy. He made the players feel good. "He's always talking to the guys about winning and believing in winning," said Lee Mazzilli, who was the Orioles manager until August 2005.

Tejada talked and joked all the time. If someone was not paying attention to the game, Tejada would yell at him. "If you're sleeping out there, he wakes you up. When you have a guy like that on the field and in the clubhouse, it makes a difference," said teammate Melvin Mora. "He's the heart and soul of this team," said first baseman Rafael Palmeiro.

Tejada has never said anything bad about a teammate. When he sees someone make a great play, he stands up and claps.

The Orioles weren't a championship team in 2004 or 2005. However, Tejada enjoyed his role on the team. Once again, in 2005 he had a great batting average of .304. He did well in the field too.

The 2005 All-Star Game was one of the highlights of the year for Tejada. That year, he did not take part in the Home Run Derby. Instead, he gave up his spot to another Dominican player, David Ortiz. He felt Ortiz was the best player from the Dominican Republic. "I think he was the perfect guy to represent our country," Tejada said.

Tejada's chance to shine came during the All-Star Game. He hit a home run. He helped the American League win the game. Afterward, he was named the game's Most Valuable Player.

Tejada poses with his MVP trophy after the 2005 All-Star Game while his son, Miguel Jr., looks on.

Tejada was thrilled that twenty-two members of his family were at the game. He was happy to make them proud. "I have to do something for my family," the shortstop said.

Although there were some great moments during the 2005 season, there were some rough spots too. Rafael Palmeiro tested positive for steroids, and in August he was suspended for ten days. At first, Palmeiro said he had no idea how the steroids got into his body. Then he said that Tejada had given him a vitamin that included steroids.

Tejada and his teammates were shocked. Taking vitamins was not against the rules. Tejada had never failed a drug test. He said he had never taken steroids or any other illegal drugs. The Orioles were angry at Palmeiro. In

Tejada talks to his teammate, Rafael Palmeiro, as Brian Roberts looks on. In 2005, Palmeiro would accuse Tejada of giving him steroids.

September they told him to go home and forget about playing for the rest of the season. No one blamed Tejada. The Orioles stood behind their shortstop. Tejada was glad for the support. However, he was hurt that a teammate could do something so mean to him.

Despite the trouble with Palmeiro, Tejada has remained the shining star of the Baltimore Orioles. He is also a shining star in his homeland. Ever since he was in the minor leagues, Tejada has sent boxes of balls, bats, uniforms, gloves, and shoes to the children of the Dominican Republic. He remembers how he had nothing growing up. "When I was coming up, you had to fight for what you had: broken shoes, no gloves," he said. "Bringing stuff over makes it a little easier for the kids."

Tejada also helped the young ballplayers by building a stadium in his hometown, Baní. In December 2004, Miguel Tejada Stadium opened. The 3,000-seat stadium replaced the rough dirt field where Miguel and his friends had played.

Tejada also takes pride in his family. His wife, Alessandra, is from the Dominican Republic. Miguel has known her since they were teenagers. The couple has two children. Alexa was born in 1999. Miguel Jr. was born in 2001.

Miguel Tejada always dreamed of being a superstar. Through hard work and talent, he has made his dream come true. He is always excited to play. "Every time I come to the field, I play happy. I have everything," he once said. "When I was a little kid, I [didn't] have anything. . . . That's one of the reasons I play so hard. I know what I came from. . . . Baseball is everything to me, every day. I love this game."

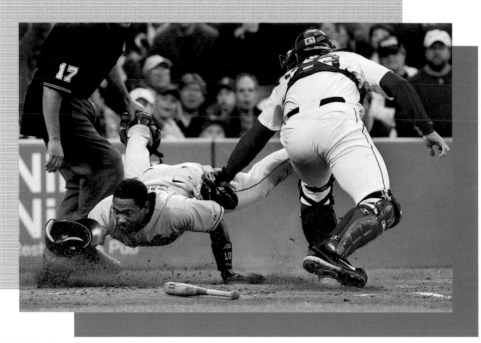

Tejada dives for home plate in a desperate attempt to score against the Boston Red Sox.

Major League Statistics

YR/Team	G	AB	R	H	2B	3B	HR	RBI	AVG
1997 A's	26	99	10	20	3	2	2	10	.202
1998 A's	105	365	53	85	20	1	11	45	.233
1999 A's	159	593	93	149	33	4	21	84	.251
2000 A's	160	607	105	167	32	1	30	115	.275
2001 A's	162	622	107	166	31	3	31	113	.267
2002 A's	162	662	108	204	30	0	34	131	.308
2003 A's	162	636	98	177	42	0	27	106	.278
2004 Orioles	162	653	107	203	40	2	34	150	.311
2005 Orioles	162	654	89	199	50	5	26	98	.304
Total	**1260**	**4891**	**770**	**1370**	**281**	**18**	**216**	**852**	**.280**

CHRONOLOGY

1976	Miguel Odalis Tejada is born in Baní, the Dominican Republic, on May 25.
1979	The Tejadas' home is destroyed by Hurricane David.
1987	Miguel leaves school to go to work.
1989	His mother dies; Miguel works in clothing factory.
1990	Miguel begins to train with Enrique Soto.
1993	The Oakland Athletics sign Tejada to a minor-league contract.
1997	Tejada plays his first major-league game.
1998	Tejada becomes the A's starting shortstop.
1999	Alexa Tejada is born.
2001	Miguel Tejada Jr. is born.
2002	Miguel Tejada is named the Most Valuable Player in the American League.
2003	The Baltimore Orioles sign Tejada to a six-year contract.
2004	Tejada wins the Home Run Derby and the Silver Slugger Award for shortstop. Miguel Tejada Stadium opens in Baní.
2005	Tejada is named MVP of the All-Star Game. With 199 hits and 98 RBIs, he wins his second Silver Slugger Award.
2006	After talk of a trade, Tejada decides to stay with the Baltimore Orioles.

Further Reading

Books

Bretón, Marcos, and José Luis Villegas. *Away Games: The Life and Times of a Latin Ball Player*. New York: Simon and Schuster, 1999.

Silverstone, Michael. *Latino Legends*. Bloomington, Minnesota: Red Brick Learning, 2004.

Works Consulted

Allen, Kevin. "Tejada's All-Around Play Sets Tone Early for MVP Night." *USA Today*, July 13, 2005.

Antonen, Mel. "Dominican President Toasts Tejada." *USA Today*, November 13, 2002.

———. "Orioles Snap Up Shortstop Tejada." *USA Today*, December 15, 2003.

———. "Tejada Blasts Way to Record Derby Total." *USA Today*, July 13, 2004.

———. "Tejada Enjoys What May Be Last Run with A's." *USA Today*, September 5, 2003.

Brennan, Christine. "Tejada's Enthusiasm Catching." *USA Today*, July 11, 2005.

Cannella, Stephen. "The Blame Game." *Sports Illustrated*, October 3, 2005, Vol. 103, Issue 13, p. 27.

Habib, Daniel G. "Miguel Tejada." *Sports Illustrated*, May 2, 2005, Vol. 102, Issue 18, p. 27.

Johnson, Chuck. "Tejada Hopes to Remain with A's." *USA Today*, February 28, 2003.

Kindred, Dave. "Enjoy the Treasure That Is Tejada." *Sporting News*, September 23, 2002, Vol. 226, Issue 38, p. 64.

Rosenthal, Ken. "Driving Force." *Sporting News*, April 7, 2003.

———. "Chirpy Tejada Keeps the Birds on High." *Sporting News*, May 20, 2005, Vol. 229, Issue 20, p. 4.

Sheinin, Dave. "Tejada's Goal for Orioles: Rule the A.L. East Roost." *Sporting News*, March 29, 2004, Vol. 228, Issue 13, p. 47.

———. "One Marvelous Maniac." *Sporting News*, June 10, 2005, Vol. 229, Issue 23, p. 40.

Vecsey, Laura. "Miguel Tejada Orioles' Enthusiastic Leader." *Baseball Digest*, June 2004, Vol. 63, Issue 6, pp. 42–44.

On the Internet

Baltimore Orioles Player Information
http://baltimore.orioles.mlb.com/NASApp/mlb/team/player.jsp?player_id=123173

ESPN.com: Miguel Tejada Player Card
http://sports.espn.go.com/mlb/players/profile?statsId=5888

Major League Baseball. "Miguel Tejada"
http://mlb.mlb.com/NASApp/mlb/team/player.jsp?player_id=123173

"Major League Baseball Events: 2005 All-Star Game." Major League Baseball
http://mlb.mlb.com/NASApp/mlb/mlb/events/all_star/y2005/index.jsp

"Miguel Tejada." *Biography Resource Center*. Farmington Hills, Michigan: Thomson Gale, 2005.

"Miguel Tejada." Wikipedia.
http://en.wikipedia.org/wiki/Miguel_Tejada
http://miguel-tejada.biography.ms/

"Miguel Tejada Biography." Biography.ms
http://miguel-tejada.biography.ms/

"Miguel Tejada Biography." JockBio.com
http://www.jockbio.com/Bios/Tejada/Tejada_bio.html

Miguel Tejada Statistics
http://www.baseball-reference.com/t/tejadmi01.shtml

INDEX